PRAISE FOR PEREGRINE NATION & LUCIAN MATTISON

"Lucian Mattison, who has lived in Brazil and Chile, takes on the role of a 'New World vulture' observing the turbulent life around him. Knives, guns, riot police, and even earthquakes are common in the Santiago of his debut collection, but there is a sweetness and sensuality to be found there as well. If 'English is a way out / tongue in which we celebrate what we leave,' Mattison's poems give us a way into "culture of silence" he so skillfully describes and disturbs. Not since the publication of Carolyn Forché's *The Country Between Us* more than thirty years ago has a poet written more compellingly about events that most Americans would prefer to ignore."

—Sue Ellen Thompson, editor of the *Autumn House Anthology of American Poetry*

"In semi-documentary dramatic scenes, Lucian Mattison tells stories about a specific locale, a peregrine nation that I can think my way into, or sink into—an outlier's view of Argentina. His scenes remain in the mind because each line of poetry, as Ezra Pound recommended, is written 'at least as well as prose.' Mattison's poetry masquerading as prose is generally straightforward but delivers sudden flips that transpose the reader to another level. He is a scrupulous poet who will engage readers with his bright, spontaneous, clear, never-strained, uncluttered, new voice."

—Larry Woiwode, Poet Laureate of North Dakota
and author of *Even Tide* and *Beyond the Bedroom Wall*

"Lucian Mattison writes poems that travel across continents and griefs, bi-cultural, speaking between languages, his is a broad geography from pool halls to the dim lights of Argentina, he brings us through the alleyways of lost loves and the bar tables where we count our losses, but always with some sense of hope, some far away music calling us as when he urges "hear my voice inhabit / a familiar melody, as if / I've lived my entire life somewhere else / in a second tongue."

—Sean Thomas Dougherty, author of *All You Ask for is Longing: New and Selected Poems* and *Sasha Sings the Laundry on the Line*

"Lucian Mattison stamps our passports and welcomes us to the Peregrine Nation, a region in history both personal and shared. Although the poems take us all over Chile and Argentina, we never feel welcome in either. Rather the Peregrine Nation seems to be a Nowhere Land for those "not completely gringo or Argentinean." By oscillating between poetic strategies, between shorter lyric and more narrative poem, Mattison formally enacts this juxtaposition, creating poetry that all outsiders will find welcoming."

> —Gerry LaFemina, author of *Little Heretic* and *Vanishing Horizon*, director of Frostburg State University Creative Writing Program

"[Lucian Mattison] demands us to pay attention to the tiny (and not-so-tiny) world of a balcony overflowing with the drama of aviary life... By casting a rich spell of image and music through each stanza, it's a risk that both pays off and delights."

> —Aimee Nezhukumatathil, author of *Lucky Fish*, *Miracle Fruit*, and winner of the Global Filipino Literary Award in Poetry

"In palpable and precise imagery, [Lucian Mattison] recounts the [...] terror that a family can experience—that's inevitable?—from a culture worn by hunger, desperation, and tragedy. The speaker's anger over the violating incident is evident as is the speaker's compassion for the other implied victims of this cultural hardship, such as the youngest son of the primary perpetuator who the speaker imagines is at some point waved "out of the dining room with a revolver." [He] seeks to not only remember an act of terror that could have become, on a mere whim, much more violent and cruel, it also speaks, through its remembering, against this terror, the "violent chorus" that results from chronic cultural hardship. It doesn't have to be this way… According to the speaker, there "everyone…looks the other way." But not here… The poem looks, and so do we."

—Amy Catanzano, PEN/Universal Award Winner and author of *Multiversal*

PEREGRINE NATION
Lucian Mattison

a **DYNAMO VERLAG** joint.

BOOKS BY LUCIAN MATTISON

Peregrine Nation

Reaper's Milonga

PEREGRINE NATION

Lucian Mattison

PEREGRINE NATION

Copyright © Lucian Mattison 2014, 2017

All rights reserved. Including the right of reproduction in whole or in part in any form.

This book was originally published by The Broadkill River Press as the winner of the 2014 Dogfish Head Poetry Prize.

This book is republished by **DYNAMO VERLAG**

Capitol Hill, D.C., Echo Park, Los Angeles, and Seattle,

Cover design by Caleb True

Author Illustration by Sarah Pfeil

Printed in the U.S.A.

10 9 8 7 6 5 4 3 2 1 blast off.

DYNAMOVERLAG.com

DYNAMO
VERLAG

ECLECTICISM | GENIUS | ORIGINALITY

TABLE OF CONTENTS

Songs for the Peregrine Nation: Obverse 19

La Noche Vieja 20

Revisiting December 2001

    Villa Miseria 23

    Golpe 25

    Martial Law 26

    Cacerolazo 27

    Christmas 28

Songs for the Peregrine Nation: Mnemonic 29

Don Gringo Speaks to a Carabinero 30

Canvas of Shields 31

Temblors

    Spring 32

    Afterhours 36

September 11, 2013: Santiago, Chile 39

A Stray in Santiago 41

Neighborhood Protest of Liceo Hannover 44

Immersion Classroom 46

Bystander Effect Villanoum 49

From the Balcony

    New Year's Eve 51

    The Earthquake 53

    The Birds 55

    Piano Rolls 56

    The Hanging Garden 57

    Bottles 59

Sopaipillas 61

Songs for the Peregrine Nation: Returning to Cordoba 63

Don Gringo and the Fireflies 66

Veo Veo 67

Songs for the Peregrine Nation: Gringo 68

The Gaucho Lectures Don Gringo 70

Driving 72

Vines and Marrows 74

To a Future Wife 77

The Payador Sings to Underground Cities 78

Epsus (The Traveler's City) 82

Acknowledgments 87

About the Author 89

PEREGRINE NATION
Lucian Mattison

From one part to the other, the city seems to continue, in perspective, multiplying its repertory of images: but instead it has no thickness, it consists only of a face and an obverse, like a sheet of paper, with a figure on either side, which can neither be separated nor look at each other.

—Italo Calvino, *Invisible Cities*

Songs for the Peregrine Nation: Obverse

I'm taught to shake out wet clothes, snap
an absent body's shape into the already worn,
my country an idea at arm's length,
distance more like an index
finger walking across a paper ocean,
map unpacked, crowded by lines and keys.

Beso a beso, me enamoré de ti.

It's easy to admire you by mistake,
regard country as a pregnant mother, her lit front
half rounded like the moon that hangs above.
Below her, we ask who drank all the wine?
What is it that actually fills her tumid belly?
A wineskin and a pioneer bloodline feel like enough
of a nation in themselves, my tongue
the billow of celestial blue pointed out to sea.

Beso a beso, me enamoré de ti.

I weigh this nation in the same way
I've approached a photograph—a miniature
woman is in the palm of my hand when, in fact,
she stands hundreds of feet behind me,
subject in the foreground, a sleight of logic,
my hand the skiff buoying the image I sing—

Beso a beso, me enamoré de ti.

La Noche Vieja

- Cordoba, Argentina 2012-13

Too few sky lanterns scatter
atop the horizon, float
above the bursts of fireworks—
shells that burn, blossom,
and fall back to earth
as ash. It's only a handful
of relatives at my aunt's.
They wait for the countdown
seated at the dinner table.

In the garden, I expand
the ribs of a paper lantern
left over from last year.
My uncle tells me
that they've been outlawed
since I was here last—
Too many fires.

I look to the sky
almost empty of them
and my memory burns
with that night, one year ago,
lit by thousands of rising
orange orbs. Flames
flickered within
these translucent papers;
our spirits sailed
over the city like fireflies.

My whole family seemed to fit
underneath my aunt's roof,
packed in tightly, dancing
Cuarteto until 4 AM,
when that one stray lantern
arrived much too late,
and nestled into the espinillo
tree in the backyard.

We all felt the fire
before we saw it spread
limb to limb. Flames licked up
from the canopy
and fragrant smoke filled the air
with the taste of camphor.
All of it was set on a canvas
of overcast, clouds the cosmic
orange of street lamps, pyrotechnic.

My cousins, uncles,
and I, all drunk
off the clock firemen, went mad
for a moment, harmoniously
putting it out
with buckets, paper cups,
the pinched tip of a hose.

Beneath the droplets
falling from the bower,
we broke charred limbs,
the badly burned, and tossed
them into the crackling grill pit.

All the while, the women
filled glasses with wine
and kept dancing.
The men flooded back in,
the crooks of their arms
like baited hooks, hands open.

When midnight vibrates
with the percussion of bombettes
and kisses each of my relatives
on the cheek, I light
a lantern's wick with a loose
match for 2013. Its hollow
gradually heats, suffuses
with a golden light
held gingerly on my fingertips.
I see through the stained paper
skin, its wiring like the ironwork
of an invisible city, no longer

with me. Release, let it rise
into the atmosphere—
palms open to the sky
in their quiet rebellion.

Revisiting December 2001

- Buenos Aires, Argentina

I. *Villa Miseria*

It's impossible to go back to the same country,
especially when some *hijo de re-mil*
puts us between two walls of an alleyway,
our hired van stuck amid a six-point turn.
We are in my mother's hands, now raised,
at the whim of eight revolvers encircling us.
The gunmen are just turning seventeen,
the youngest maybe thirteen like me.

It's a shame I feel lucky
that one of these thugs rips open
the passenger side door, jams his revolver
into my mother's ribs, grabs both of her breasts
just for the fuck of it, and after stripping us
of everything we have, asks another revolver-
waving kid *Y que hacemos con ellos ahora?*—
as if he were tormenting a passel of farm hogs.

I feel lucky that they ran out of fresh ideas,
that we were left with our lives.
I often think about revisiting that alleyway
and how things would be now.
I see half of them pass a broken *bombilla*
between them, inhaling whatever charred hope
this country proffers in a fifty peso note
stapled to a ballot slip. I see them crumpled
like soda cans in a canal, riddled

with some other street kid's bullet holes.
Look down this barrel,
this country's empty wine cask,
see God's bloody handprints all over the walls.

II. *Golpe*

Looking through the window of the backseat,
I see the son of a bitch giving orders—he smiles

a rack of impacted teeth growing out of the top
of his gums, as if a second mouth bites through

to supplant the old. Where is he now—belly full
of red meat, waving his youngest son

out of the dining room with a revolver?
I hear him tap his muzzle on the table

as he wonders why he didn't take the van,
complete the illusion, at least make it seem

like that driver might also lose
some essential piece of himself out there with us.

But we both know the driver will do it again.
Everyone here looks the other way.

III. *Martial Law*

It runs on a loop—a horse cadaver crawls
with insects, a supermarket vomits hordes
of looters, banks all have broken windows,
police sit with their hands tucked beneath
their backsides, mouths stuffed with rubber
bullets—
the images lull a mother and son to sleep
in television light. Locks on the windows,
doors bolted shut, the father has fallen asleep
in a plastic chair before the front door,
hand on the loaded pistol in his lap.

IV. *Cacerolazo*

It sounds like the city is being overrun
by an approaching caravan
of silver and soda cans: violent chorus,
empty hollowware beaten

with wooden spoons, iron stock pots
cast through the windows of cop cars.
The noise amplifies in the canyon
of concrete apartment buildings—

a third president in five days, the Casa Rosada
permanently flushed pink with shame.
The nation is going hungry for a fifth
day straight, but everyone sings,

pushes against the traffic on Santa Fe,
pushes toward that little pink house
even though most of them know
it's been empty for a long time now.

V. *Christmas*

At about four AM the fireworks
peter out, and the whole city
is suspended in moonmilk.

Nobody in this apartment is sober,
except for my mother,
and she holds her brother's head

over a toilet bowl. Stumbling in the belly
of the living room, I spin
my cousin's petite frame, as *Discovery*

cycles through its third play,
the only CD in the apartment—
a gift from my brother. My sister

smokes on the balcony because she's 15.
It's impossible for me
to understand how fucked up

this country has become.
I am holding my eyes open
with a beer bottle.

Songs for the Peregrine Nation: Mnemonic for Argentina's Invented Currency

Lecop is the tourniquet for La Nación
Patacón a wound exposed to Buenos Aires.
Cecor is the loose suture holding Córdoba
Federal's currency floating Entre Ríos.
Cecacor tells us Corrientes is running dry,
Bocade Tucumán is an empty mouth.
Quebracho's worth bark peel in Chaco,
Boncafor, Formosa's foremost IOU.
Petrom fills the barrels in Mendoza.
Bono Público a brand name for Catamarca.
Boade Serie A relegates La Rioja's futbol team,
Huarpes the virus San Juan keeps secret,
and the other Patacón 1 shoe missing
hobbles the last horse in Jujuy up North.

Don Gringo Speaks to a Carabinero

The officer holds a spoon in his right hand, *touch it*.
I do.
He throws the spoon into the ocean, *go fetch*.
(The spoon is still in his right hand)
He asks me why I'm not retrieving it from the ocean.
I ask him if he really threw it.
He tells me to go find it and tell him.
I walk into the ocean and search.
I can't find it.
I pull a scallop from the surf and bring it to him.
He runs his fingers over the ridges.
He confirms this is the spoon and throws it back.
He tells me to go find it again.
I walk into the surf and find a cockleshell.
I bring it to him.
He says a shell is a shell—I shouldn't lie to him.
He tells me to throw the shell back into the ocean.
I throw it like he says.
He asks me why I threw the spoon into the ocean.
He says, *fetch it. I can cuff a gringo just as fast.*
I see the outline of the spoon in his pocket.
I turn out the white tongues of my slacks.
He slides his hand onto the handle of his club.

Canvas of Shields

                    Santiago, Chile, 2012

Scarfed students throw sawed-
off plastic bottle halves
of turquoise, crack
carabineros on helmets, drip
celestial hues down plexiglas
shield partitions. Every soldier
is up to his knees in acrylic—
splatters of stars, splotch
of Pollux, mantled
cosmos over batons—
rainbow of *No*
cast across riot gear.
Masks weep onto olive drab,
bleed a city's changing colors
from clothes to street, soldier
to art student, mouth
defiantly opening—distorted
metropolis, expressionist
uniform the new canvas.

Temblors

I. Spring

A guest in their house,
        I've been mostly quiet.
They sit cross-legged
        in the courtyard:
his mother in a gunmetal
        dress, military father
stiff as old oak, and left-
        leaning eldest son,
Martin, lifting a cracker.

Aspic jiggles on its dish,
        as the rumble
of the day's earthquake
        stops conversation,
titters a butter knife
        on a paté dish,
the shells of licorice-
        mint clams on Pyrex.

The father asks me
        to watch how the wine
in my glass trembles
        with the quake,
no matter how still I think
        I can hold it.
Looking into the bulb,
        I begin to read myself
on the wrong side

        of an Allende novel,
gringo in the open arms
        of Pinochet's hangover—
Chicago Boy laying *el ladrillo*
        down over the cordillera,
from *Republica* all the way
        to *La Reina*.

The mother presents
        a photo of Martin
as a small child. His face already
        stamped with adult
calm, the copper streaks
        in his shoulder-length
hair like buried lode.

        Martin never once looks
at me as they fawn over
        this image. I'm in awe,
equal parts admiration
        and terror at how
they don't seem to care
        about the faults
that quiver aftershock,
        tectonic masses
reluctantly coming together
        beneath our feet.

A condor circles above.
        I wonder if it also
recognizes that the world
        is shaking? Can it sense
how scared so many people
        still are of this presence?

It lands on a limb overhead,
        tremors subside.
The New World vulture's
        eyes glisten, wattle
a bulbous mass like the jowls
        of old age. I see
the same growth hang
        below the father's
cracked, purple lips, a deformity
        that comes with knowing
more than one lets on,
        acting as if nothing
about the scene is off.
        I won't dare
question them about lineage,
        what years saw them
into the wealth surrounding us,
        or if the marriage
of regime to mountain ore
        was all arranged
from the chefs all the way
        to the bedroom.

The Peruvian cook brings out
        a topped tureen,
aji de gallina stewed
        in almond cream,
ladles portions onto our plates.
        I pick up my fork,
eat quietly, my spirit bound
        under the silence
of a knowing bird above us,
        trembling lode
within the surrounding hills.

II. Afterhours

Martin guards his coffee when he speaks, says
someone like me, not all gringo or Argentinean,

is a good thing in Chile—*just know when to play
the right hand.* Framed in smoke and red laser lights,

the waitstaffs' dayglo thongs reflect endlessly
in the mirrored walls of the café con piernas—legs,

bare breasts become bytes of my pornographic
memory. He tells me our server, Nata,

will be a nurse after university.
Once she's hired away from the café for good,

he'll be perpetually sick. We tip her outrageously.
The taper of her eyeliner winks a silent, *todo cambia,*

menos los hombres—this Cleopatra of the Catolica
de Chile behind tinted windows. Slaked

thirst and drunk stumble, Martin and I
head downtown from the West side

toward the quiet of the Moneda Palace. All around us
the streets are littered with lemon wedges, torn

garments, and fractured glass after the day's protests.
The walls are dreamscapes in spray can letters—*fuera*

Monsanto, Pinochet and president Piñera painted
side by side. Martin closes up like a clam

when I grip the barriers before the palace and yell
as loud as I can, *Piñerachet, chupa-culo de los gringos.*

He shoots glances in every direction, unnerved
by the absence of police. He tells me to quiet down,

that we shouldn't draw any attention
without more people as witnesses. I'm split in two,

one half wanting to continue to yell, the other asking
whether or not they would club a gringo

and a politician's son. For the first time, I see real fear
on Martin's face—how he must have looked

when his mother held a single finger to her lips,
pointing upward to heaven as if to say, *Quiet,*

He hears everything. Maybe it's the drink talking,
I tell him to yell with me as we walk by the capitol,

whatever he can muster at staircases, concrete
fountains, locked revolving doors. He gives in

and what comes out shakes me—an Andean gale
laced with strange curses: *pacos chuecos,*

fascistas caraduras. A heavy rain begins,
pours over my nose. We pick up our pace.

A police siren approaches. It feels right, so I ask
if he feels any guilt being his father's son.

He says, *The whole sky is coming down
into this porcelain cup of a city,* pats my cheek

a little too hard with his right hand, *you can't argue
with a pistol or a copper mine.* At this point,

we're wearing the weather inside our boots.
My whole body shakes uncontrollably,

vision leaving me. Martin grabs my arm, glances
over his shoulder. It could be the shakes,

but I see policial lights flicker on the church wall
beside us. He tells me that we need to run.

September 11, 2013: Santiago, Chile

- 40 year anniversary of the Chilean coup d'état

Two kilometers of students lie head
to toe in a line along the sidewalk
of a busy street. Backs the ground, they keep

an eye on the crowd of spectators.
Today, eleven minutes of silent demonstration
is time enough to make headlines, enough

time to ask that my Northern half recognize
our invisible hand guiding the knife—
how we carved a wound in the Andes,

let people disappear before we called it *terror*.
This human scar, out in plain sight, cuts through
the heart of the city, a single motionless line

of people from the Plaza Italia, downtown
to the Moneda palace steps, those same steps
where Allende was sh—

                                      shot himself.
I realize, to those students streaked across
the pavement, even my voice has a double,

an emblematic bird and its dark shadow
that swiftly caresses their bodies from above.
My breath is the wind lifting the New World

vulture—just a whisper below the skin
of a cicatrix. I wish more of us could mourn
with them, but then again,

how are we supposed to remember a headline
that never made it in our papers? We never
even needed to try to forget.

A Stray in Santiago

'73 marked the last
stroke of a switch,
permanently landing
a dog's tail
between its legs. Pinochet
leashed his terrier
to an almond
in the palace courtyard,
where dogs of all
kinds lay bloody
on the steps.

Head bowed
between two limbs,
it genuflected, outstretched
toward his feeding
hand. It was '90
when he finally unloosed
the puzzled creature;
below the bower
it woke and slept
as if still tied up,
gagged by overcast skies
corking the cordillera,
its hind quarters
sitting in a puddle,
rain reflecting it all back
in a shade of gunmetal.

Years passed, the dog
roamed underground
tunnels on a diet
of rat, chasing trains
back into subterranean
galleries where
they're stored nose
to tail—thousands
of dogs asleep
in defunct carriages.

In time it shed
the invisible whip
held over its head,
sharpened its teeth
on the rolling stock,
reconditioned. The last time
it was seen, it slept,
again near the almond
outside Moneda Palace,
but hundreds more
like it were turned askew
on cardboard box mats
surrounding the building.

And tonight,
all of their legs twitch
in dreams
like at the tail end
of batteries, kick
at the air, these upturned
toys waiting for him

to appear, his image
in a phalanx
of riot police, leash
in hand. They can smell
the metallic tinge
of blood on batons,
beneath fingernails,
still feel the pull
of invisible cords,
not yet dead inside
of them. They know
they are too many
this time
and yet, they each fear
equally, shiver
in a light sleep.

Neighborhood Protest of Liceo Hannover

- Municipalidad de Maipu, Santiago (2011)

In a matter of days, avocados
fell from above, unripe, picked
from a nearby tree, and launched
over the school's fence.
Fruit collected atop goal nets,
streaked viridescent across windows,
bruised aimlessly. Teachers
and parents gingerly picked them up
like defused grenades,
held them for all to see—
halt classes, demand the tree
be felled—as if the solution
were to extend a chain link
barrier up three meters
on all sides, and reopen the doors.

And for two days the fruit stopped,
and everything continued
as before, until one lunch
amplified into recess and store-bought
Pura Crema Palta rained down
overripe like gobs of green
pulp from a canopy line.
It was mythic—decaying fruit
materialized as if from prayer,
bursting neon on contact,
one hitting a thirteen-year-old
girl squarely in the eye,

her screams aimed at the *nobody*
that blinded her.

Teachers lifted her limp
body, held their hands over her
hands, pressed them to her face,
all these clenched fingers caked
as if stopping her green spirit
from leaking out of the wound.
Above the tears, insults cursing
the *flaite* trash that wouldn't last
a day in private school, hung a veil
of awe—how these kids
still continued to fill their fists
with something like flowers,
and opened them again
to reveal a grist of bees—
how they scattered in the air
above everybody's heads.

Immersion Classroom

They model verbs,
fill their mouths
with insoluble

sound, shape
the perfect loops
of their lips

around vowels,
always notes off-
key, but tuning

cords taut.
It's progress
I hope

I make
each time I tie
a half-Windsor

knot wayward,
slight tail
to the left

indicating the years
between us
I can count

on one hand. I try
not to breathe out
the previous night's drink.

Drill—*listen
and repeat*—fumble
subjunctive,

show up unconjugated,
pillow case
of tousled hair

atop my head
for a handful
of secondary

students, who without
fail, undo the tangle
I keep trying

to perfect—bijou
from polyester
on my voice box.

They ask, who
taught you to tie
that *huevada?*

Like calling trumps,
I answer, *ask
me in English*,

hand shielding
my sour breath,
this currency

against theirs,
every word tightening
inside my throat.

Bystander Effect Villanoum

He uses the same words: *por favor, ayudame*
auxilio, rising from the deserted street below.
People are asleep or wait for somebody else

to act. After two minutes of the assault, he still begs
for the mugger to stop—for anyone in Santiago
to notice. He uses the same words: *por favor, ayudame,*

auxilio. I pretend to sleep—everybody motionless,
next to lovers, insignificant others, a whole barrio
of people in the dark, waiting for somebody else.

It only gets louder, crescendos with each kick,
pleads through audible tears—my eyes close,
repeating the same words: *por favor, ayudame.*

It only gets louder, his crescendos with each kick
to the ribs, asking this culture of silence
with the same words: *por favor, ayudame.*
I just wait for it all to be stilled, voice to peter out

within his ribs, infected by this culture of silence.
Nobody moves or even dials a number.
I just wait for it all to be stilled, the voice to peter out
like all of us in our beds pretending to sleep,

as nobody moves or even dials a number.
We ask the same thing, wait for somebody else,
all of us in our beds pretending to sleep,
using the same words: *por favor, ayudame*.

From the Balcony

Santiago, Chile (2011-12)

I. New Year's Eve

Mortars light the night sky and for hours
the city has become a bandshell of concrete
apartments. The square below saturates with patter
of student shoes, tire smoke billows over the tops

of buildings, and everything smells of torrefied
minerals. We're on the top floor, most American,
all of us temporary or scared enough to know
not to get involved. My balcony looms above

the streets, where just hours ago the whole city
was flooded with pots and metal spoons. Crowds
gathered outside *La Moneda*, face-to-face with riot
masks, and beat a metallic hymn at the seemingly

ancient structure. I was on the outside, apart
from this new backdrop for the city: barred doors,
streets littered with lemon wedges, the dialogue
of bodies growing each day, and the arriving trucks.

From my balcony, I saw sections of protesters
fall back like ebb tide, every inch of their bodies
soaked by the spit of water cannons, as stray dogs
leapt into the streams, baying in ecstasy.

White gas jetted from armored cars, the toxic
contrail shepherding the droves of those fleeing

like insects from an orchard. I remained
on my perch, black anorak draped over me,

a New World vulture waiting for everything
to settle. I burned through cigarettes, watched
the subway entrances inhale tear gas, all of it
slow and dreamlike, as if nitrous were spilling

over the city's lips. Hours passed in a deep
afternoon sleep and midnight approaches. The city
reawakens with songs that inflate the air
with student buzz. People serry in the streets drunk

with passion, as their parents could have only
dreamt of doing after '73. Carabineros get dressed
in the plaza, batons and masks, their turtle shells,
and they fuse together to usher in the inevitable

New Year's violence. My guests hurry in
from my balcony. We seal ourselves off again
from the outside. Our countdown is followed
by the shatter of beer bottles at the feet of police.

Clouds of tear gas rise up into sky, leak into cracks
around the doors and windows. We touch
champagne flutes, eyes bloodshot and acrid.
A local asks where I keep my lemons. *Why* hits me

a little late, as she quarters them, hands out slices.
We murmur with them between our teeth, children
breathing through strange regulators, all of us
holed up inside, until our throats stop itching.

II. The Earthquake

The last time the whole city
        blacked out. The earth
finally coughed a lung
        after years of the mantle's
hiccups, and only then
        did people ask after
their neighbors. Two weeks in,
        I felt my bones
hollowing out, a procession
        of vulture feathers
sprouting on my arms.
        From a solitary window
I roosted over Alameda's
        sprawl, reclined on the twin
mattress of a rental,
        cradled a prepaid phone—
just texts and a few drinks
        from a retreat
into the cursory comfort
        of an expatriate's open legs.

It must have been
        how starved I was,
but when my bed began
        to shake, I thought
—muffled hostel sex—
        my neighbors engaging
in an urgent silence
        like drunk foreigners
on the bunk below.

       I let the bed totter some
semblance of me,
          until I slid the door
to my balcony, open
       stepped outside half-
nude onto the ledge to see
        it wasn't just my room,
but the whole city shaking.

       Bare back to the glass,
I froze. My hands grasped
       for anything solid to hold.
It's coming from Valparaiso,
       a local college student told me
from the adjoining balcony
       after the trembling stopped.
I said I'd never felt one
       before, my body still stuck
to the glass like a dead insect.
       She lit her cigarette,
We tremble the same
       no matter where we are.
Was it that different?

III. The Birds

Sparrows nest in the puddled iron latticework
of the balcony next door. Birdseed carpets

the floor and spills onto the street below.
The residents seem to be on endless holiday
because the birds come and go as they choose.

They dig their talons deep into their feed,
carelessly spill it over the ledge, or tamp it

down as if it were a bank of trampled snow.
They even sleep in their food, husks of split seed
coats stick in the crooks of their wings, bits

hovering slipshod atop feathers. Santiago
should be iced over this time of year.

The birds fly away when I walk outside to shake
a cigarette from my pack. They quiet and watch me
from a nearby almond branch: hulking animal,

a song in foreign smoke, condensed milk breath,
my egg-tooth glowing red between my lips.

They huddle, wait until I stomp out the cinder
and slide the door closed. The world resets.
By the window, I listen to their voices kindle

and rise back into song. Breasts puffed,
they hum as if filled with buff-tailed bees.

IV. Piano Rolls

The balcony belongs to a bedridden woman, guilloche
ironwork holding plaster walls in place like a back brace.
You can hear a song whenever the tawny nurse opens

the sliding glass door. It's like peeking into a music box—
the melody follows the Peruvian outside
as she smokes or hangs a bedspread out to dry.

Today, a song spills over the rails like a sheet roll
around the gears of a pianola. It bounces and warps
off concrete walls of the surrounding apartments,

each note tripping on the wind's phantom fingers
in plinks like muffled pizzicato. The sopranos go silent
and the deep C falls off the edge of the body out of tune.

The pinblock peels, maple discolored like thrift clothes,
keys tucked into the bed, swept across a face, yellow
as old teeth. The music stops when the glass door clicks

back into its frame. Even after the nurse leaves,
her tureen piping a contrail of steam behind her, I wait
like this woman, in and out of sleep, for a melody.

V. The Hanging Garden

The spiderwort
dangles into the balcony below,
their hearty stems
sundried horse leather.
They shoot out in all directions
searching for a nook
to grab a foothold
along the ironwork.
A hose leaks
onto the street below
and passing pedestrians
look up past the building's wall
to the clouds.
The youthful widow
spends hours knitting
on the balcony,
her plants twined
over the rust railing.
The ferns, bindweed,
and upside-down tomatoes
hang from the ceiling
like a veil. They cast her
every pull of thread
and fabric loop in the verdant
shade of nacreous jade.
Sometimes the breeze
draws aside the vines
like bedroom window blinds
and for a moment
you catch a glimpse of her,

sprouts of crow's feet
branching out from her eyes,
the slight jerks of her swelled arms,
weaving and counting,
and the unraveling skein of yarn
that quivers beside her,
a single egg
endlessly trying to hatch
in a clutch of woven wool.

VI. Bottles

There are so many she can
hardly stand outside. In lines,
like cigarettes in a fresh pack,
spent liters of lager press flush
with one another from the wall
to the balcony rail. She leans
back against the sliding glass door,
a tesserae Madonna, corona
in amber and reflective glass.
Over weeks of grey weather,
I see her bottles fill.
The furthest from her door brim
like rain gauges, silhouettes
of brown liquid gradually falling
lower the closer to the door
the bottles are. I measure
her days in languor, my water
clock the centiliters of rain
that creep up an *Escudo's*
glass curves. My months
steadily drip from the broken
faucet in my kitchen.
I speak fluid ounces, pottles,
or liquid scruples, measurements
I can't express in my second tongue.
I grip the rail, stumble
through vernacular with Mario,
my housemate of six months—

even we feel miles apart.
We're both on the balcony
when she appears this time.
It's like watching a hummingbird
through a kitchen window.
She holds her gaze upward,
splaying a black mantle of hair,
her eyes chrysanthemum
buds half-closed. I tell
Mario, *ella tiene piel*
como leche de almendras,
when I really mean to express,
there is never enough time
with her, nothing more
luxurious than drinking her
figure in with a glass of wine,
or dreaming of her fingers
caressing the nape of my neck,
her mouth drunk from my lips.
As if she can hear my thoughts,
we lock eyes across the avenue,
both of us six floors up,
apartments face-to-face.
A drop of rain
taps the tip of my lit cigarette.
She tips a bottle back,
drinks, leaves
one more empty at her feet.

Sopaipillas

Santiago, Chile

Michael and I start at the corner
of *Paris y San Francisco*, hit #202
in *Lastarria*, then enter the bar district
as long as our wallets can last.
I've won and lost so many friends
in this same way, tabs paid,
the coins left in my pocket
refusing to take me home.

We flock to these makeshift deep-
fat fryers, twelve gallon stewpots
strapped in shopping carts.
They pepper sidewalks near the mouths
of metro stations, oil smoke
frying the air, puffing up sopaipillas,
pastries stacked in piles
like second-hand saffron flat caps.

Chilly wind at our backs, heads
slush-filled fishbowls on our shoulders,
we post up, hands to the heat,
fish 100 pesos from our coat pockets,
fill up on squash bread heaped
with *ají*. His Brogue, my Yankee,
both gringo, lost on vendors.

They hand us our street
communion, labor of nocturnal priests,
tempered gold pieces
hailing our confessions: how moving
homes is an afterthought, distance the only way
we justify treating everyone we meet
abroad like cobblestones.

For us, English is an escape,
tongue in which we celebrate
what we leave, staying out
until subway trains yawn with students
on Thursday morning. Suits,
stained cargos emerge from doorways,
hightail it toward the carts,
sopaipillas now breakfast
tickets skewered on a metal spine.

Pressed between sunlight
and sleep, in the subtle bubble
of salamandrine fryer heat, we return
to our own beds on the bus
line—split at Paris
and San Francisco. The pit of my belly
churns the grease, hastily filled
like a suitcase of unwashed clothes—
knots me up with an image just like this,
weeks away, a hurried embrace
before I open a taxicab door,
say, *aeropuerto Arturo Benítez*.

Songs for the Peregrine Nation: Returning to Cordoba

is recovering
a large stone
submerged
in the *rio segundo*.

You swim out
in December,
humidity
resting enormous

paws on your shoulders.
Sub-equatorial
glacier melt
swells the arroyo,

as you float
just toes
above this oblong
shape, temporal

lobe steeped,
a piece of you
immersed
in the valley's tannins.

You fill your lungs
with *Cimarrón*
steam, valley
drawl the cold

drink on your tongue
when you dive,
lift the abraded
rock from the bed,

walk this heavy
thing to shore,
and drop it
on the sand.

You scrub away
a coat of algae
with a bunched up
shirt, the stone

gathering heat
from the sun
before you rest
your head

on its smooth
curve, afternoon
sleep taking
you. It's rising

that first morning,
cheeks kissed, eyes
half open, lard
pastries like little books

in a bread basket—
the waking body
a kettle
singing on the stove.

Don Gringo and the Fireflies

Cordoba, Argentina

Dusk swarms with the heavy breath of ash-
fires among the leaves. Back in the country

of my mother's birth, I try to mimic them
as I breathe in my own glow, a cigarette

trapped between my lips. It was here
my mother once told me,

the fireflies are spirits, our dead
family members alive in the tails of insects.

I was six, holding my father's beer can. He smoked
to the filter, tossed the *bocha* with the other hand,

stamped out his cherry cinder. I pointed
to the smudge of sylph, memory on his boot,

and asked him how many he'd held,
how many he'd put out in his life.

Raising a fresh cigarette to his lips,
he quieted me and kissed two fingers—*too few.*

Veo Veo *

- La Boca, Buenos Aires

Que Ves?
Contours of coastline,
la plata's rust cloud of algal
bloom, *matanza* steeping
a shipyard in ribbons of oil film,
Caminito's dump, jetsam and fishhooks—
una cosa—rumbled mélange of wordless
roar, melody swirling, cosmic,
semblance of song materializing like cumulus
overtop *que cosa? La Bombonera. Maravillosa,*
the spare Mortise key in pocket—open
that door on Avenida Rocha, glide through
the intestinal hallway of my deceased
grandfather's building, up to the slit-
hatch spy hole revealing a single
scanning eye—*de que color? Latón
pulido*, locked in that split
second of recognition, my
first cousin's pupil
dilating.

* A call and response children's game similar to "I Spy"

Songs for the Peregrine Nation: Gringo

I watch tio Charlie hunch over
a Spanish guitar, yaw,

his jaw wide with *El Canción
de Las Cosas Simples.*

I follow his fingerpicking, strum
with a cigarette, voice flickering

like the call of a Sickle-
winged Nightjar. When he sings,

I see my grandfather's moustaches arch,
eyes bulge, a song erupting

from both men at once.
His chest puffs up, bellows

for lungs, and blows outward
through grease smoke, links of blood

sausage hissing, his mouth a grill
chimney spitting it out

over the crickets. It's always
after dinner, late into the night,

when I finally sing along—*que el amor
es simple, y a las cosas simples*

las devora el tiempo—hear my voice
inhabit a familiar melody, as if

I've lived my entire life somewhere else
in a second tongue.

The Gaucho Lectures Don Gringo

Your blood is not of here
anymore.　　　　It stinks of

The States (bringing a fist

down
onto the table, he startles

the wine glasses).

Your Hollywood teeth
nauseate me,
　　　　　　　that tongue isn't
rolling properly anymore.

Don't you feel at all

　　　　　　　　ashamed?
Let me remind you

that you are just one person
no matter where

you find yourself.
As opposed to many,

you might say?
　　　　　　　You are like me

of this I am certain.

(He picks a beetle
off of his sleeve
          and presses

the creature between thumb

and forefinger) I know
how you grow weary

of putting on so many voices,
portmanteau   of faces

like folded   laundry, lists
     of people you keep

leaving behind. See
for yourself.   Sleep

one more night
among your insects

up North   and tell me

you have not yet been bitten.

Driving

Drunk, I feel my way by boorish
        hands, sleepwalk
into a vehicle—turn
        the key. A heartbeat
pulses in the flooded paw prints
        of my eyes, the spirit
behind them holed up elsewhere,
        feet still wet.

        Asleep at the wheel,
I veer between points
        on a country—a cloud
of bonfire smoke
        from her hair, mineral taste
of Cordoba's tap water
        on her lips, grape
seed oil beneath
        her fingernails—place
that leaves me like a slow leak.

        I wake in strange places,
rooms behind me mantled in dark
        matter barely visible
in starlight, so I can't recall
        where I've gone,
my life made up of memory,
        all these blind spots—

        tracks from absent animals
I fill with my feet,

          faint memory of a swerve,
a doe in the mirror standing
          on the side of a country road,
her image behind me,
          getting smaller.

Vines and Marrows

- Cordoba, Argentina

Six year ago, my senile
    tía Leticia stood at a dinner party
        and recited Tango verses about a crookneck

vine that bore sundry marrows.
    One of the two remaining sisters
        of the 13, husband gone, solitude

sprouted into the air
    around her. The dinner table
        welled up with her tears. She produced

a silence, so palpable, we bathed
    her in a nonplussed applause.
        Her eyes, a pair of calyces and brindled

irises, were wide open
    like a newborn's, as if she were
        desperately refilling them with cimarrón

dust, a pitcher of red wine,
    cognac and oranges, the faces
        of a family she could hardly recognize.

•

I see my mother, twenty years
   from now, companionless, her bones
         like cast-iron and her heart a heap

of eggshells. She shuffles inside
   her pristine home, cooks for four,
         and recites fragments of Neruda

to herself —*Comer solo es amargo*—
   as she stirs a nickel spoon in a bowl
         of mariner's soup. She prepares

her yerba mate, twists open a bag
   of lard pastries when she phones
         to remind me that it's November,

that she invited the whole family
   next month. She's already planned
         every meal, rearranged the furniture,

swept out the guest bedroom.
   I have to switch off my phone at night
         to keep from picking it up the fifth time.

•

The last of the sisters, Utto, died last month,
   each woman alone in her last years, my blood
         tells me that husbands expire before wives.

I look to my left atrium to see my father's
    heart failures, on the other side the genetic
        disorder of my mother's maiden name, Diaz

—Parkinson's buried beneath it.
    I don't want to vanish a decade early
        like all the men in my family. I wish

to have a woman who swells like those
    on my mother's side, her skin hardened
        like winter gourd, swallow's song emanating

from within until her last breath. I want to pass
    around the *yerba mate,* sip from the silver straw,
        catalogue the family with her, a grandchild's

birth like refilling a bowl of tea with steaming
    water, my hands around a steeping bloodline,
        drawn from the same calabash gourd.

To a Future Wife

I would prefer you die ahead of me,
your skin stiff, bloated plump like a bagpipe;
me as gourd, the pulp of life overripe,
still tethered to vine, curing among weeds.

If sixty-six is anywhere in years,
add twenty more without you at my side:
I swell, vinegar-filled like a horsehide
wineskin; crosswords carpet my floor, ink feet;

my nails curl monthly into boot toe steel.
Nights are rotgut in distiller's retorts,
drunk in front of a mirror, just the Lord
and I in evensong—His piggish ear
in my cornmeal, our scrapple mass deep fried.

No, I'd prefer to be the first to die.

The Payador Sings to Underground Cities

Buenos Aires, Argentina (2012)

Gusts of wind cudgel the clouds, hack
at the sky's seams, and frostbitten
moons fall onto the earth. They hit
the windows, cracking on contact
with balconies, and coat the pack
ice on the city streets. Downtown
saturates with its winter sounds:
boots on concrete steps, the grinding
coffee beans, thunder chattering
bowls of snifters hung upside-down

in a corner bar, as the ranks
of busses snort their diesel lines.
Up an avenue, I take flight,
my anorak billowing black
like condor wings in the updraft.
I descend into my pool hall—
El Aro—I've spent much too long
in this place, tired of the hailstones,
this endless storming that follows
me down the pockets where I fall.

After Santiago was Sao
Paolo, leaves later, I riffle
through sheets of bound pages, still
adrift in the larger novel.
Instead I tail an icy pearl,

as it tumbles from the heavens,
down a staircase toward the tavern,
and into a glass of sloe gin.
The percussive storm's muffled din
patters overhead, and the whir

of the basement fan steadies my
heartbeat, tunes me to the quiet
of the poolroom's own dialect—
whispers of smoke swirling at eye-
level across the hall, the sighs
after strings of pocketed ducks,
a day-old bar glass being unstuck.
At home in the metal reed notes
of *Complaint of the Bandoneón*,
I feel the passionate squeeze of

Piazzolla's bellows bending
through a Victrola horn, its lilt
like caressing a table's felt.
Manu, my friend with the missing
index finger, begins speaking
volumes. It's as if only here
he feels he can. His energy,
invisible at the surface,
builds as he fiercely polishes
the tip of his cue beside me.

He's hushed, hides his face when he lines
up shots or makes mention of his
mute son. Some days sticks fly, fists
strike the table. He cues holes, eyes

in the drywall for each loss at nine
ball. He leans, draws his arm back, cocked
like a wound tension spring, and shocks
the rack with every ounce he can
muster. Highs and lows scatter and
agitate, some lucky ones drop

together, others stop dead near
the opposite end, stragglers stay
in the kitchen. He works his way
encircling the table. Like me
he's mid twenties, hard to believe.
Between the angles his eyes weave
combinations, almost like he's
picking a lock, picking his life
apart since he swelled up his wife
with twin boys at just fifteen.

He tells me he walked out on one
stillborn. For the other's lost voice,
he faults guilty seed, his choices
this virus inside a woman.
I keep my turns short, simply done,
only relaying anecdotes,
that in comparison, just don't
hold a candle to what he's gone through.
He tells me I'm one of the good
ones, a feature rare for gringos—

really all he can hope to find
is a proper woman and friends
to listen beneath this endless

noise that spackles cracks in our lives.
I tell him that we're all contrived
fictions, our heads these big cities
that we build—how so frequently
they collapse atop us outside
the pool room. He says, *no surprise
that you keep noticing me here.*

I see people live underground
all over, men who sink themselves
into what they've come to accept
as home. Even if briefly, we're found
in these pockets speaking the sound
of muted cracks, unwitting kiss
shots punctuate cue balls—English,
bottom left. We listen hard to
the grind of chalk dust that drops blue
snow on our hands, the ponderous

thunk of change trays, coins pushed in,
disarming tables. Words pour out,
collect inside the open mouth—
We reach in, rack them up again.

Epsus: The Pilgrim's City

From a distance, the city appears
to be a giant banyan tree. The traveler

approaches to discover her walls
are blanketed in vines. They root

into the city floor, create what seem endless
hallways of vertical stipes.

The abundance of food in Epsus
is the most striking of all its qualities,

the whole city consisting of traders
calling out to foreigners and argosies of merchants.

Arcades brim with tumescent fruit.
The streets have become so littered with peels

and seeds that each traveler is responsible
for beating the roads upon which they walk.

If you ask someone who lives there
if anyone ever goes hungry,

they will look at you dumbfounded,
as the word *hunger* has changed its meaning;

yet, ask them which foods they take
pleasure in and they will look at you

with the same inscrutable stare.
They do not enjoy the zest of fingered citron

on carp, nor the taste of any
of the thousand strains of melon and plum.

Each person keeps a single plate,
fork, and spoon,

and rarely invites guests for meals.
Rather, there is a tradition that has developed

in Epsus, one of fasting for weeks at a time.
There are communal longhouses

built specifically to bunk
those who wish to fast together.

Only in the sport of starvation
is any true desire for food expressed.

Those who participate paint still lifes
of human bones and vegetables,

fashion lemons out of the wax
from their ears, dye clothing

in the pigments of plant matter.
This mad desiring and worship

of their city's produce only persists
until the fast is broken.

One eats with displeasure
that which is placed in front of her.

Those who don't die of old age in Epsus,
perish from the ongoing competition

between hunger artists,
each attempting to out-starve the next.

ACKNOWLEDGMENTS

Grateful acknowledgment is made to the following publications in which some of these poems first appeared: *Barely South Review* (Section III of "From the Balcony"); *Country Dog Review* ("Songs for the Peregrine Nation: Gringo" under the title "First Generation Argentinean American (Gringo)"); *The Flagler Review* ("Sopaipillas"); *Hinchas de Poesia* ("Songs for the Peregrine Nation: Mnemonic for Argentina's Invented Currency"); *Muzzle Magazine* ("Don Gringo and The Fireflies"); *Post-Pravda* ("Canvas of Shields," "La Noche Vieja," and "Spetember 11, 2013: Santiago, Chile"); *Poetry Quarterly* (Sections *I* and *IV* of "From the Balcony"); *The Poet's Billow* ("Vines and Marrows"); *SLAB* ("Revisiting December 2001") and "The Payador Sings to Underground Cities" in *Double Kiss: Writers on the Art of Billiards* (Mammoth Books, 2017).

Thank you to Amy Catanzano for selecting the poem "Revisiting December 2001" as the winner of The Elizabeth R. Curry Poetry Contest and to Larry Eby for selecting "Vines and Marrows" as the winner of The Bermuda Triangle Prize. Thank you to the judges of the Dogfish Head Poetry Prize,

Diane Lockward, Gerry LaFemina, and Larry Woiwode.

Special thanks to Luisa Igloria, Tim Seibles, Remica Bingham-Risher, and the faculty at Old Dominion University. Thank you to my teachers and ODU MFAs that offered their continual support and encouragement during the creation of this book. A special thank you to Michelle Bonczek, Matilda Cox, Sean Thomas Dougherty, Robert Evory, Katy Hurston, Michael Khandelwal, Dorainne Laux, Karen An-Hwei Lee, Mark O'Connor, Evie Shockley, Andrew Squitiro, Taylor Stevens, and CLB.

And the utmost gratitude to my family, Maria, Bill, Ben, Camille, and my extended family in North and South America, whose boundless love and support made this book possible.

ABOUT THE AUTHOR

Argentinean-American poet and translator, Lucian Mattison (Los Angeles, CA, 1987), is the author of two books of poetry, *Reaper's Milonga* (YesYes Books, 2017) and *Peregrine Nation* (Dynamo Verlag, 2017), winner of the 2014 Dogfish Head Poetry Prize. His poetry, short fiction, and translations appear in numerous journals including *Hayden's Ferry Review*, *Hobart*, *Muzzle*, *Nano Fiction*, *The Nashville Review*, *The Offing*, and *Waxwing*. His poems have won the Puerto Del Sol Poetry Prize, The Elizabeth R. Curry Poetry Prize, and have been nominated for the *Best of the Net* Anthology. He received his MFA from Old Dominion University in 2015. He currently works at The George Washington University in Washington, DC, and edits poetry for Big Lucks.

DYNAMO VERLAG BOOKS

Telescopes and Other People
JOSH NORMAN

The Ramayana of Valmiki: The Chrystal Verses
ANDROS CHRYSTAL

Chansons Russes
CALEB TRUE

Peregrine Nation
LUCIAN MATTISON

DYNAMOVERLAG.COM

www.ingramcontent.com/pod-product-compliance
Lightning Source LLC
Chambersburg PA
CBHW060536080526
44586CB00012B/757